Mighty Mountai
Swirling Seas

Poems by Valerie Bloom
Illustrations by Alessandra Cimatoribus

Contents

Forest 2

River 3

Mountain Volcano 4

Valley 5

Blue Mountain 6

I Am a Wall 9

In Yellowstone Park 10

Mountaineers 11

Potholing 12

Rivers and Streams 15

The Mountain and I 16

No More 17

The Angry Sea 18

The Ocean 20

Bored 23

The Little Stream 24

Come to the Lake 26

Rainforest 28

The river's journey
    to the sea 30

Collins

Forest

Forest.
Home to Baboon,
Elephant, Leopard. The
Giants of the jungle. And home
To ants.

2

River

River,
Moving cargo
In barges to the sea,
Pounding rocks, destroying homes, and
Singing.

Mountain Volcano

This is
The giant that
Sleeps, gentle as a babe,
Until anger like a fountain
Erupts.

Valley

Sitting,
A referee
between hills which once were
One. Peacemaker, keeping them from
Clashing.

Blue Mountain

All night we climbed the mountain,
Excited in the dark,
The flare from the small lamps up ahead
Looked like a tiny spark.

We reached the top just as the sun
Was wiping the sleep from its eyes
And sending out red fingers
To investigate the skies.

It suddenly leapt out of bed,
Wrapped the world in an orange flame,
And we gasped in wonder at the sight,
This was why we came.

We watched the shy blush spread across
The face of the bashful sky,
We saw the cars like tiny ants
In the roads below, crawl by.

We heard the birds chirp awake,
Saw them flit across to plunder
The rose-apples and the hog-plum tree.
Heard a waterfall roar like thunder.

We washed our faces with the dew,
Breathed the perfume of the Four O'Clock,
Watched a lizard climb a stone to sun itself,
Then scuttle away in shock.

We headed back down the mountain,
The sun was wide-awake and bright,
Our legs were tired and heavy,
But inside, our hearts were light.

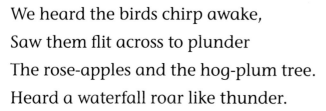

I Am a Wall

A riddle

I am a wall, sheltering you from cold,
I am as ancient as the world is old,
I am a fountain from which springs are born,
I am mother, nursing the wolf cub and the fawn,
I am a building, a sturdy tower of strength,
I am a backbone, measuring the earth's length.
I am a guard, keeping watch on high,
I am a giant finger, pointing to the sky,
I have a foot, but cannot move,
I own a heart, yet cannot love.
What am I?

A mountain

In Yellowstone Park

In Yellowstone Park big-horn sheep roam,
Here bison and bobcats have their home,
There's the grey wolf and the grizzly bear,
Mountain lion and white-tailed deer,
Coyotes and chipmunks, elk and moose
Fishes, snakes and the Canada goose.
Bald eagles and osprey, loons and hawk
Live happily together in Yellowstone Park.
I don't think that these animals know
They're living on top of a volcano.

Mountaineers

We've got our boots, we've got our packs
Up the mountain we go.
A slip, a slide, a rumble, a thud
And watch out down below.
We climbed the mountain fast, and then
Even faster, we're down again.

Potholing

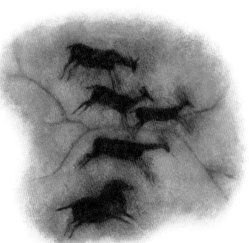

We're going in a grotto,
We're going in a cave,
We're going to learn about the way,
Cave animals behave.

We will need some tall boots,
A jumper to keep us warm,
We'll go deep inside the cavern,
To watch those columns form.

We might see some swallows,
We might see some bats,
We might see a raccoon,
Some bobcats or pack rats.

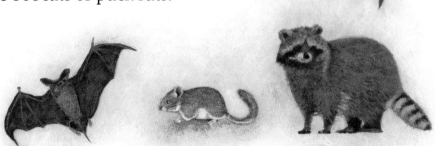

If we go a little further,
There might be crickets and flatworms,
I hope you're not scared of spiders,
This is where they make their homes.

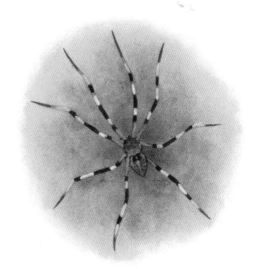

But you needn't be afraid,
For I'll be there with you,
I will show you where to go,
And I'll tell you what to do.

We'll go into the darkest part,
It's pitch black everywhere,
You don't want to lose your lights,
When you're going under there.

We may wade through waist-high water,
We may climb a rocky wall,
We may need to get on all fours,
Lie on our bellies and crawl.

We sometimes squeeze through tight spots,
You can't always run around,
When you go potholing,
In a big hole in the ground.

Yes it might be cold in there,
But it will be so much fun!
You go on, follow the guide,
I'll join you when I'm done.

Rivers and Streams

The hungry rivers wandered,
Through the mountains they meandered,
Then smelling food, they rushed, and gushed, and swirled.
Gorging themselves on the mountains
They cascaded down like fountains,
And carved out the great canyons of the world.

The little streams rambled,
Through the knolls and hills they scrambled,
Peering into all the hill's small nooks and niches,
Nibbling on the rocks and stones,
Like puppies chewing on their bones,
They dug out all the world's gullies and ditches.

The Mountain and I

I sit at the foot of the mountain
And gaze at the azure sky
And no one sees the sky's sorrow
Only the mountain and I.

I walk by the side of the mountain
And watch a small stream flow by
And no one hears what it whispers
Except the mountain and I.

I climb to the top of the mountain
Up through the forest so high
And we listen to the mountain's heartbeat
Just the mountain and I.

No More

No flying frogs glide, no parrots shriek
No crowned eagle with its curved beak

Circles the canopy, looking for food
No woodpecker drums on the mahogany wood

No snake curls around tree bark
No tree frogs sing out after dark

No marmoset builds its nest up high
No giant trees reach towards the sky

No orchids bloom up in the tree
No sloths crawl by, slow but free

No monkeys swing from branch to branch
Raining down fruits like an avalanche

No jaguars hunt on the forest floor
There is no forest any more.

The Angry Sea

Today the sea is angry
She's pounding the cliff's face
And all the birds that live there
Have been driven from their place

Today the sea is angry
She's striding up the beach
And she's chewing up and spewing out
Everything within her reach

She's battering the shoreline
And in her violent rage
She's snarling like a lion
That's been locked up in a cage

Today the sea is angry
And with her massive waves
She bites big chunks out of the rocks
Leaving underwater caves

Today the sea is angry
Someone has made her mad
Her face looks dark and glowering
Like when I've upset dad

Today the sea is angry
But I'm safe here on the shore
I'm just sorry for those fishes
Who have made the sea so sore.

The Ocean

The ocean's a lapdog
Licking my toes
And chasing the seagulls
The pigeons and crows.

The ocean's a pirate
Boarding boats with his waves
And burying his loot
In undersea caves.

The ocean's a builder
With seashells and sand
He builds towers like mountains
On the face of the land.

The ocean's a teaser
He lays gifts on the beach
But when you try to collect them
He draws them out of reach.

The ocean's a sculptor
And he carves out in stone
Faces and buildings
And creatures unknown.

The ocean's a drifter
Over rocks and on shore
He roams about knocking
On each country's door.

The ocean's a postman
And year after year
He brings messages in bottles
To folks everywhere.

The ocean's a parent
Tending to the wishes
Of sailors and bathers
Birds, whales and fishes.

The ocean is busy
He's got so much to do
But he's never too busy
To listen to you.

Bored

I'm bored and unhappy, the mountain said,
Winter's arrived and the birds have all fled,
Snow clouds are gathering overhead,
I think I'll put on my ice-cap,
Get under my ice-sheet,
And go to bed.

The Little Stream

The little stream wanders
Twists and meanders
It's searching for something
What can it be?
It looks under stones
Sifts through dirt, grime and bones
And its soft song is tinged with misery.

It meets other streams
Chasing their dreams
It joins them and together they travel and search
Under banks, under bridges
Over steep mountain ridges
Looking under the roots of willow and birch.

The little stream's stronger

It's grown wider and longer

But still it's not happy, its song seems to say,

I've looked high and low

Does anyone know

If I'll ever find it? Will I find it today?

The little stream's rushing

Its waters are gushing

In urgent cascades as it comes round the bend

And it shouts out with glee,

"I've found it! The sea!

My searching has finally come to an end!"

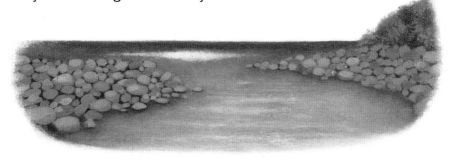

Come to the Lake

Come to the
Lake and the
Herons will
Fly

Look at the
Water as
Blue as the
Sky

Count all the
Geese as they
Honking pass
By

And push your boat on the water

Come to the
Lake as the
Meadowlarks
Sing

Look at the
Swan as he
Struts like a
King

26

Feed all the
Ducks with the
Bread that you
Bring

Then jump in your boat on the water

Come to the
Lake as you
Slip from the
Shore

Feel the soft
Waves on the
Boat and the
Oar

Drink in the
Peace and your
Spirits will
Soar

As you row your boat on the water.

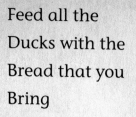

Rainforest

There is a place where it rains a lot,
Where trees grow straight and tall,
This is the place where the sun shines hot,
And the howler monkeys call.

There is a place where fallen leaves
And tree trunks cover the ground,
This is the place where the wet soil heaves
As beetles scamper around.

There is a place where banana trees,
Giant figs and palm trees grow,
This is the place where you can feast on lychees,
Avocados and juicy mango.

This is the place where the orchid blooms,
Home of toucan and macaw,
The capped heron with milk-white plumes,
The green snake and black mamba.

There is a place where folks make their home,
Where they hunt and fish and farm,
This is the place from which medicines come,
Which heal diseases like a charm.

This is the place that is trying
To survive the tractor's roar,
This is the place that is dying,
A place that will soon be no more.

The river's journey to the sea

31

Ideas for reading

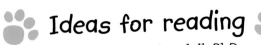

Written by Clare Dowdall, PhD
Lecturer and Primary Literacy Consultant

Learning objectives: read most words quickly and accurately, without overt sounding and blending, when they have been frequently encountered; discuss their favourite words and phrases; continue to build up a repertoire of poems learnt by heart, appreciating these and reciting some, with appropriate intonation to make the meaning clear; explain and discuss their understanding of books, poems and other material, both those that they listen to and those that they read for themselves

Curriculum links: Geography, Art and design

Interest words: mighty, swirling, pounding, clashing, bashful, gorging, azure, mahogany, glowering, honking

Word count: 1623

Resources: pens and paper, ICT or other riddle poems

Getting started

This book can be read over two or more reading sessions.

- Hand out the poetry books and look at the covers. Ask children to talk about their experiences of visiting and seeing mountains and the sea.

- Discuss the title *Mighty Mountains, Swirling Seas*. Ask children why these adjectives have been chosen and what pictures and feelings they create.

- Turn to the contents. Ask children which titles appeal to them and why.

Reading and responding

- Turn to pp 2–3. Read the poem "Forest" aloud. Ask children to say what they think is special about the first three giant creatures described e.g. *they are beautiful, magnificent, majestic.*